LITTLE BOOK OF

TOM FORD

First published in 2024 by Welbeck
An Imprint of HEADLINE PUBLISHING GROUP

1

Cataloguing in Publication Data is available from the British Library

ISBN 978 1 80279 648 3

Printed and bound in Italy by LEGO SpA

HEADLINE PUBLISHING GROUP
An Hachette UK Company
Carmelite House
50 Victoria Embankment
London EC4Y 0DZ

www.headline.co.uk
www.hachette.co.uk

LITTLE BOOK OF

TOM FORD

The story of the iconic designer

KRISTEN BATEMAN

WELBECK

CONTENTS

INTRODUCTION

Tom Ford changed fashion as we know it. Not only with his namesake brand, but also with his brilliant stewardship as creative director at Gucci and Yves Saint Laurent.

The designer started by revolutionizing the house of Gucci, bringing it up to modern speed with fashion that shocked, excited and delighted on a global stage. Think: velvet suits, visibly exposed G-strings, and a knack for dressing everyone from Madonna to Gwyneth Paltrow and Beyoncé. From 1994 to 2004, Ford worked as the creative director of Gucci, and when Gucci acquired the house of Yves Saint Laurent in 1999, Ford was named creative director of that label, also until 2004. At Gucci, Ford turned the business around and saved it from near bankruptcy, catapulting it into a global success internationally with his designs, which pushed at the boundaries of conventionalism but also offered up a radical dose of powerful sex appeal so specific to Ford.

Ford was vastly ahead of his time. The key to his work being an eye turned to subverting gender, bending the perceivable rules and thus shedding the shackles of fashion rules. Pinstripe mobster suits for women? Yes. Little underwear for men on the runway?

OPPOSITE A young Tom Ford with a model wearing his debut collection for Perry Ellis America, 1990.

Yes, again. "Often I get the question 'Why do you put makeup on guys?'" Ford noted in an interview for *The Advocate*, in 1997. "'Are they trying to be more feminine?' or 'Why are you showing masculine suits on women?' I hate those two words, feminine and masculine. I mean what are they? Why is a suit masculine and not feminine? And why is eye makeup feminine and not masculine? It's so stupid. We're just people. The guy has eye makeup on so he's more beautiful."

His influence spanned far beyond Gucci, however. At Yves Saint Laurent, the designer turned a historical brand set heavily in the past into something new: taking references from global cultures and the Ford aesthetic to bring forward silky renditions of YSL classics. There were stunning white versions of the signature Le Smoking jackets, plus a nod to the romanticism and imagery of travel that Yves Saint Laurent himself once instilled into the brand. Plus: furs, jewel tones, ornate buttons, feather trims, lush contrasting colours and dramatic proportions all at once. While Ford's Gucci put a cheeky 1970s spin on the 1990s streamlined minimalism that was seemingly everywhere, Ford's Yves Saint Laurent veered fast in the other direction and faced glamour head-on.

By 2006, Tom Ford launched his own dazzling menswear, beauty, eyewear and accessories line under his own name. And with it, he riffed on many of the house codes that he had revolutionized at Gucci and Yves Saint Laurent. Ford told *CNBC* that the Tom Ford customer is "international, cultured, well-travelled, and possessing disposable income" and "strong women, … intelligent women who know their own style".

What sets Ford apart from many contemporary designers of today, too, is an ethos and aesthetic that defines a lifestyle. His homes, his campaigns, even the way he himself dresses is Total Ford-ian from head to toe. Usually in a suit, and more often than not, wearing his signature 1970s-inspired aviator sunglasses, which

can be seen so often in both his womenswear and menswear collections for his namesake brand. "I was born in a jacket," Ford told the *New York Times* in 1996. "I was the only three-year-old who walked around with a blazer folded over his arm. I was very particular and very difficult, and I would only wear certain shoes. When my mother would go out, I would move the furniture and rearrange the living room. I just wanted to redecorate the world."

In November 2022, the Tom Ford brand was purchased by Estée Lauder for $2.8 billion, and *Forbes* estimated that the designer would earn $1.1 billion from the deal. In April 2023, he stepped down as the brand's creative director and was succeeded by Peter Hawkings, adding that his next creative foray would be intrinsically tied to film. It's an area Ford has already explored, through his own film production company, directing *A Single Man* (2009) and *Nocturnal Animals* (2016). The sheer force of impact Ford has created throughout his career is matched by few designers. The future undoubtedly holds more for him.

TOM FORD
AT GUCCI
AND YSL

PUSHING BOUNDARIES

At the 1995 MTV Music Video Awards, Madonna proudly accepted her award while wearing a striking bodycon teal-blue satin shirt and low-slung trousers. "What was she wearing?", reporters asked. Her answer: "Gucci, Gucci, Gucci." It was, in a single word, groundbreaking for the future of fashion since Gucci itself had previously only been associated with leather goods and handbags. Tom Ford invented the language of Gucci's clothing.

The son of two realtors, Tom Ford spent most of his early life in Houston, Texas and Santa Fe, New Mexico. But even when Ford was a child, he knew he had a taste for aesthetics. His grand visions and specific tastes would lead him to study interior architecture at The New School's art and design college in New York City, Parsons School of Design, from where he graduated with a degree in Architecture. After an internship at Chloé and a two-year stint designing at Perry Ellis, Ford got the call to join a crumbling Gucci in 1990.

OPPOSITE Madonna at the 1995 MTV Music Video Awards, wearing the infamous blue satin Gucci shirt designed by Tom Ford.

For four years, he spent most of his time working behind the scenes. But his success was lightning quick: he jumped to designing menswear within six months, quickly followed by shoes. In 1994, he was officially named the creative director of Gucci with the support of rising new chief executive Domenico De Sole, eventually overseeing everything from ready-to-wear collections to fragrances, image, advertising and store design.

In 1993, Gucci lost $22 million on $230 million in sales due to licensing. Revenues in the first nine months of 1995 doubled, to $342 million, over the previous year. But by 1999, Gucci was valued at more than $4 billion. Ford famously worked 18-hour days, and when he left the company in 2004, Gucci reportedly had to hire four people to replace him.

The secret to Ford revitalizing Gucci was this: creating a new intrinsic language that was so in your face, so glamorous and so steeped in sex, that the world couldn't wait to get its hands on it. Gucci had previously been known as a brand strictly concerned with leather bags, shoes and silk scarves, but now, season after season, Ford unveiled a new, covetable item: bodycon cut-out jersey dresses, logo bedecked G-strings or jeans covered in beads and feathers. Looking to the archives for any kind of inspiration, Ford was met with old Hollywood stars like Elizabeth Taylor carrying leather bags. He decided in turn to subvert the idea of celebrity through runway shows, focusing a single spotlight on models as each one paraded down the runway. For fashion shows at this time, it was a very specific and dramatic look.

Ford brought hedonism and a certain kind of ostentatiousness back to fashion in a sea of formal, rigid minimalism. In 1994, for his debut as Gucci's creative director, Ford presented the world with the Gucci clog in pink, beige and black as well as the infamous Gucci loafer, now with a sexy stiletto. White mini shift dresses with voluminous pleats sealed the deal.

OPPOSITE Gwyneth Paltrow's red suit designed by Tom Ford for Gucci for A/W 1996, which she wore to the VMAs, was an instantly iconic moment in fashion history.

OPPOSITE In 1997, Jennifer Lopez showed the slick, minimal, sexy side of Tom Ford's Gucci designs, in a backless black slip dress.

RIGHT Lil' Kim makes a statement in Tom Ford for Gucci A/W 2000, featuring micro hot pants, a glittering top and white jacket.

But it was 1995 that marked Tom Ford's first fully designed Gucci collection, after Dawn Mello, the former vice president and creative director who originally hired Ford, left the company to join Bergdorf Goodman as president. The industry had decided: Tom had arrived, and in 1995 he brought with him a new kind of Gucci like no one had ever seen before. Amber Valletta, Shalom Harlow and Kate Moss paraded down the runway for the Fall 1995 show in luscious jewel-tone satin button-downs, velvet hip-huggers, and vibrant chunky woollen coats and furs in acid shades of tangerine, chartreuse and moody shades of celestial blue. The other half of the collection was saturated in rich black and brown suiting, with low-cut tops, slim leather jackets, chunky furs and tightly cut, short suiting for men. Most models on the runway were without the major item the House of Gucci clung to: bags.

It was a very big year for the designer, who not only showed his new vision of Gucci as sparkling, glamorous, a little bit mysterious and very commercial – but also formed distinctly directional visual partnerships that would endure throughout the rest of his career. Take, for example, Carine Roitfeld, the one-time editor-in-chief of *Vogue Paris* and legendary stylist he brought on to style his shows, and Mario Testino, the Italian photographer he tasked with shooting his highly directional, risqué campaigns.

By Fall 1996, Ford was able to lean even more into his bohemia-fuelled sexy '70s aesthetics by creating an entire collection that revolved around slick jersey dresses with cut-outs, belted cat suits and pinstripe suiting. It was, as *Vogue* dubbed it, the "fashion equivalent of a one-night stand at Studio 54", and the references to some of the greatest designers of the '70s – specifically of New York City, like Halston – were very much present. It's no surprise: when Ford was a student, the iconic disco club Studio 54 was one of his hangout spots. There were luscious jewel-toned suits, cut-outs carefully placed near erogenous zones, glamorous old-world outerwear and tops that went down to there.

RIGHT Tom Ford proves his devotion to glamour in the form of this bright yellow Gucci look worn by Mary J. Blige at the 2004 Grammy Awards.

These codes would remain ever-present, not just at Ford's souped-up Gucci but also later when Ford would go on to create his namesake brand. Ford's signature beauty look was born during the Fall 1996 collection: hair slicked tightly back with smouldering dark black eyeshadow and chiselled cheekbones. The faces of Ford's Gucci convey notions of both strength and androgyny and take cues from the beauty looks of silent film heroines. Gucci finally had a narrative, and Ford stood as its great storyteller of epic proportions.

The young designer was often thinking in broad terms of uniforms when he was designing for Gucci in his early days. "That's the way I live and move, and that's why the uniform idea is important," he told the *New York Times* in 1996. "Everyone dresses in uniforms now. It's for people who live an international life. That's our customer."

Ford's Gucci also felt new because it was so different from the house's former reputation, far and away from the tradition of leather handbags and silky floral scarves. Ford experimented with accessories in a different way, integrating them directly into clothing. Take, for instance, glitzy medallions drawn from the historic horsebit, shining metal chains in between jersey cut-outs, and small and neat "G" logo belts. And while Ford espoused total glamour, the commercialism that lay deep within his work is what made it appeal to the masses. These were clothes anyone could aspire to wear – to the office, for a night out, or anywhere – just as long as you could afford them. They were wearable in a way that other contemporary, intellectually avant-garde designers of the '90s weren't.

By 1999, Ford was still pushing his idea of hedonistic 1970s glamour, though with a slightly different spin. It was much more Bob Mackie than it was Halston, with Cher serving as the inspiration du jour. Gucci's Spring 1999 ready-to-wear collection, presented in October 1998 in Milan, was all in favour of the

OPPOSITE Kate Moss walked the runway for Gucci's A/W 1996 show, designed by Tom Ford.

LEFT A glamorous chartreuse gown from Gucci's A/W 2004 collection, the last Gucci collection designed by Tom Ford.

OPPOSITE A minimal look with business-like trousers and a logo-G string peeking out, from Gucci's S/S 1998 collection designed by Tom Ford.

Summer of Love, expressing that same 1970s sentiment but in living colour, borrowing heavy embellishment and surface decoration from Indigenous and African craft traditions. There were psychedelic floral dresses, little fringe skirts, sheer sweaters and denim decked out in lush feather trim, beading and embroidery. *Vogue* called it the collection with the "decade's most-wanted jeans" and Ford told the *Los Angeles Times*, "These are eclectic, eccentric, and – I hate to use the word – happy clothes." Meanwhile, Ford continued to carry some of the same themes through in his menswear collections. Celebrities couldn't get enough either.

Once 2000 hit, Gucci was poised to take over as one of the most powerful fashion houses in the world. Gucci received a $3 billion cash infusion, which led to the takeover of Yves Saint Laurent in a $968 million sale in 1999. The new creative director of the brand? Tom Ford, who would also be the first designer to design under the Yves Saint Laurent label besides the founder himself.

So divisive were the tensions between Yves Saint Laurent the man and Ford that Saint Laurent reportedly skipped out on attending Ford's runway show debut for YSL. In attendance were emblematic icons of the house, such as the YSL muse Betty Catroux, a friend of the designer's since the 1960s, and Pierre Bergé, Saint Laurent's partner of 40 years. And yet, Saint Laurent himself flew to Morocco for the occasion, famously citing Ford's work: "The poor guy does what he can."

Ford was set on creating a collection that was as far removed from Yves Saint Laurent's ethos and aesthetic as possible. Like wiping the slate clean, he offered up a mostly all black and white collection with wide cut pants, barely any accessories, and pointed shoulders. Ford eschewed all the typical house codes and references formerly associated with Yves Saint Laurent. And at the same time, it was also something newly distinct and different from what he built his name on at Gucci. "What he

OPPOSITE Another striking acid-hued, absinthe-coloured look from Gucci's A/W 2004 collection, showing Ford's innate sense of high-octane glamour.

LEFT Tom Ford taking his victory lap for Yves Saint Laurent's A/W 2004 collection, his final collection for the house.

LEFT Tom Ford's debut collection for Yves Saint Laurent was presented for the S/S 2001 season – and offered up a new, minimal vision of the brand.

wisely chose to do was please young, world-weary women whose idea of Saint Laurent is not a safari jacket and thigh-high boots, the epitome of 70s cool, but rather a new thing – a slouchy white tuxedo with wide, cuffed trousers and a tight top scooped low enough to suggest a cummerbund," wrote Cathy Horyn in her *New York Times* review of the debut show.

He was quick to differentiate YSL and Gucci, telling *Harper's Bazaar* at the time that the difference under his direction was that: "They may both be beautiful and they may both be roughly the same age and they may both have money and they may both be sexually available. But the Gucci woman is sweeter, more naïve. She may be like, 'You're a great guy, let's fuck.' The Saint Laurent woman is more twisted, more perverse. She is going to tie you up and slap you around before she finally lets you have sex with her. And a lot of that doesn't come so much from Yves, it comes from all those provocative Helmut Newton pictures of YSL clothes from the 70s."

Still, the YSL years for Ford may have been overshadowed by his own work at Gucci, but there were a few bright moments that left their mark on the fashion industry forever. For example, YSL's Mombasa bag. With a chunky, crescent-like shape, the bag came in beautiful leathers and had a hefty handle made of wood, metal and horn depending on the model. It first launched in 2002 and was reportedly gifted to Gwyneth Paltrow. According to the *New York Times*, the bag was quick to sell out and gain a competitive waiting list, resulting in YSL selling $90 million of accessories, accounting for 26 per cent of total sales.

At both Gucci and Yves Saint Laurent, Ford had a hand in creating must-have covetable accessories. At Gucci, he reintroduced the Jackie bag in 1999 and the brand reportedly sold a million. At YSL, what made Ford's contribution so especially profound was that the brand had no accessories portfolio (other than costume jewellery) prior to Gucci acquiring it and bringing him onboard.

Ford would end up leaving both Gucci and Yves Saint Laurent in 2004, but not before having an epic year. In 2003 alone, Gucci stores in the United States hit an all-time high, selling nearly $4 million in a single day on 4 December.

And yet, internally at Gucci Group, rumours were swirling. By November 2003, Tom Ford and Domenico De Sole announced they would be leaving the company. The duo decided not to renew their contracts with Gucci's parent company, Pinault-Printemps-Redoute. While Ford declined to comment on the reasons for their departure at the time, sources reportedly said that it came down to control. Despite all this, Ford maintained that he would still design the Gucci and YSL Fall collections shown in 2004. These would be his last shows for the labels.

In his final year at Gucci and YSL, Ford continued to push the boundaries at both brands. Particularly at YSL. Ford seemed to be getting more comfortable with the codes of the house, and started experimenting more with the exuberant and daring dashes of crazed colour so signature to Yves Saint Laurent himself. At first glance, Ford's work for YSL seemed much more conservative than what he was doing at Gucci, but upon closer inspection it was easy to see those subtle Ford-isms that riffed on surprising sexual innuendos. Nipples were painted dark blue to become more visible under clothing (and sometimes peeking outside sheer layers) and models were decorated with penis necklaces.

His Fall 2004 collection for Yves Saint Laurent was one of his most exciting with pagoda shoulders, rich jewel tones and a plethora of chaotic, clashing colours that represented Ford's mastery of the YSL palette. It was inspired by Yves Saint Laurent's 1977 Les Chinoises collection that coincided with the launch of the fragrance Opium. "I felt the pagoda shoulder was right. And it was a period I hadn't mined," he explained.

OPPOSITE Tom Ford focused on creating his own aesthetic for YSL, as seen here for the S/S 2001 collection – and only reinterpreted very subtle house codes of the past.

OPPOSITE Tom Ford upped the kink factor with a sculpted bust breastplate complete with a pierced nipple for Yves Saint Laurent S/S 2001.

RIGHT Black and white was the main colour palette for Yves Saint Laurent S/S 2001 collection, eschewing the bold hues and vibrant jewel tones of the founding designer.

LEFT A bondage-like effect was created through the use of strappy black fabrics in Tom Ford's Yves Saint Laurent S/S 2001 collection.

For his final collection for Gucci, Ford pulled out all the stops with a memorable finale. Rose petals fell from the sky as he ascended for his final bow; 'Nothing Compares 2 U' played over the speakers. The collection represented a curation of greatest hits. Think: slinky white dresses with elegant cut-outs crafted with oversize metallic jewellery. Then there were new iterations of the very first blue velvet jackets of 1995, as well as a slew of other pieces that had previously been seen on the runway. Beaded pants, white coats and every kind of exotic material and fur imaginable. Crystal-covered gowns dazzled under the light. But the jersey dresses were some of the most iconic. Modelled by Gucci campaign girl Georgina Grenville, they resembled the styles from Gucci's Fall 1996 collection. Ford showed us every shade of red-carpet outfit possible through candy-coloured floor-length feather dresses, shimmering sequined halterneck dresses in lime and cobalt and black bondage style dresses with sheer panelling.

As a co-ed collection, he featured men on the runway in streamlined suiting, neat little bow ties and scarves thrown over their necks. And then there was also the hair and makeup which represented not only the iconic era of Tom Ford's Gucci, but the underpinnings and makings of an entire world of aesthetics come to life. Slicked back hair parted to the side, dark black eyeshadow applied liberally and smudged, a light nude lip, a strong but somewhat bleached brow, and as so often, aviator sunglasses.

Vogue's Sarah Mower wrote of Ford's final Gucci collection, "There is no doubt who the Gucci woman is: the embodiment of sexual confidence, burnished to a high gloss and bursting with predatory power. A symbolic figure of the past decade's hedonistic highs, she spike-heeled her way down a runway carpeted with pink fur, luxuriating in Ford's aesthetic one last time." While the famed fashion critic Cathy Horyn of the

OPPOSITE Tom Ford's menswear designs share similar aesthetics with his womenswear work.

RIGHT Tom Ford's 2004 Yves Saint Laurent collection was inspired by Yves Saint Laurent's 1977 Les Chinoises collection that coincided with the launch of the fragrance Opium.

RIGHT An icon of design from Tom Ford's YSL era is the Mombasa bag. With a chunky, crescent-like shape, it launched in 2002.

OPPOSITE Tom Ford played with elements of bohemian style at Yves Saint Laurent, as seen with this peasant-style blouse.

New York Times wrote, "In one of the classiest presentations of his career, Mr. Ford showed them how it was done. This was big-time fashion. From the first exit to the last, there wasn't an outfit that looked wrong, a hair out of place. The clothes reflected not only the high points of his career, but also his ability to project an idea beyond the small, limited world of fashion."

It was the end of an era, sure, but Ford would be sticking around in fashion for the long run.

TOM FORD AT GUCCI AND YSL 41

OPPOSITE Tom Ford takes a bow after one of his shows, as seen with his life partner Richard Buckley.

RIGHT The actor Julianne Moore, a friend of Tom Ford, wearing a Yves Saint Laurent dress designed by Ford at the 2003 Academy Awards.

THE BEGINNINGS
OF TOM FORD

DRESSED FOR SUCCESS

Hot off the heels of leaving Gucci Group, where he served as creative directors of both Gucci and Yves Saint Laurent, Ford founded his own highly anticipated brand in 2006. But it wasn't without a little side project involving star-studded celebrities and high-octane glamour first.

Ford served as the guest editor for *Vanity Fair*'s annual Hollywood issue, acting as a curator of sorts, and placing Scarlett Johansson and Keira Knightley on the magazine's March 2006 cover. The designer was incredibly forthcoming about his upcoming fashion line, teasing it to press almost as soon as he left Gucci, so the *Vanity Fair* opportunity felt like a stepping stone to the wider launch.

Unsurprisingly, Ford's self-titled line, Tom Ford, was founded with former Gucci Group CEO Domenico De Sole, often credited as one of Ford's biggest champions and long-term partner in Gucci's success. He would now serve as Tom Ford's chairman. Ford initially launched his brand with menswear,

OPPOSITE Friend and client Daphne Guinness, pictured with Tom Ford, wearing one of his designs for his namesake womenswear label.

ABOVE The first stand-alone Tom Ford boutique opened in New York in 2007.

OPPOSITE Tom Ford's early menswear collections were heavily influenced by suiting and 1970s glamour.

beauty, eyewear and accessories – which were first available at the initial Tom Ford store on Madison Avenue in New York City. With immaculate tailoring and sharply cut men's suits being the major fashion focus for Ford, it made sense to partner with an established manufacturer that had a long history in the industry. Thus, Ford linked with the Ermenegildo Zegna Group to produce and distribute the new line. The Italian luxury fashion house was founded in 1910 by Ermenegildo Zegna in Trivero, Biella, in the Piedmont region of northern Italy.

The store, where many would have the opportunity to see Ford's first pieces for his namesake line for the very first time, was much more of a quiet luxury aesthetic than the high-powered glamour Ford showed at Gucci and Yves Saint Laurent. In fact, it was incredibly understated: most of the interiors were grey while glass cabinets held the clothing as if

they were museum pieces. The walls were suede-covered and the distinctly chosen Italian cabinets and a wet bar (drinks counter) nailed the details that Ford was so obsessive over. Eschewing feminine glamour, Ford's store was almost entirely full of men's suits that often fetched $5,000 – more even, if you wanted something custom – which left many of his female customers, fans and the general fashion press frankly wondering why, as well as what was next.

Still, Ford's ethos as a designer and for the overall Tom Ford brand was shown in this very first store: "In a Savile Row firm, for the same price, you might be standing on a plain box for the fittings. No extras, no romance, no butler to offer you a Scotch. Of course, the plain box doesn't diminish the worth of the suit, but what do the little extras actually provide? An authentic experience? A balm for the ego? Security, the sartorial equivalent of a gated community? It is perhaps a simplification, though not much of one, to say that this kind of cosseted shopping experience reflects a growing rich/poor gap that has been scarcely acknowledged in fashion (except to fuel it at the upper end)," wrote Cathy Horyn, after visiting the store for the first time in 2007.

Very early on, Ford had the support of top-tier male celebrities who opted to wear his clothing at his profile events or in even more high-profile films. One such instance was Daniel Craig, who wore Tom Ford for his final four James Bond films, first in *Quantum of Solace* (2008) and later in *Skyfall* (2012), *Spectre* (2015) and *No Time to Die* (2021).

Soon enough, the Tom Ford line would find a bigger platform through wholesale. By 2008, the luxury department store Bergdorf Goodman (just a stone's throw from Ford's own shop in Midtown Manhattan) would open its own Tom Ford shop-in-shop, the first retailer to stock the brand. At the time, it was touted as the biggest in-store boutique that Bergdorf's

OPPOSITE Tom Ford also designed menswear collections at Gucci, pictured here. This work later informed his own line.

had ever done in the men's department, and it also included fragrance and accessories.

The next year, in 2009, the Tom Ford company announced that it was finally time to launch its long-awaited womenswear chapter. Tom Ford International was seeking investment of more than £30 million to begin producing womenswear.

Almost one year later, in 2010, the label would debut its first womenswear collection in September. It was a very big deal not just for Ford himself and the company but for the general fashion public and the press. Here was a designer who had been one of the most highly regarded creative directors of his time, lauded for his genius ability to bring something to fashion that felt like a spiral of newness with passionate energy. He had made his biggest impact at Gucci and Yves Saint Laurent through womenswear, and the world was now

ABOVE Daniel Craig wore Tom Ford in his series of James Bond films.

OPPOSITE Many of Tom Ford's menswear designs at his own label were inspired by his work for Gucci, such as the metallic suit and bow tie, seen here.

waiting with bated breath to see what, exactly, would be next when Ford stepped out into womenswear on his own for the very first time.

It had been six years since Ford last designed for women, when he left his post at Gucci Group – and Ford wanted to do something really special for the occasion. In lieu of holding a massive show packed full of thousands of guests (reminiscent of the Gucci heydays), Ford narrowed the guest list down to roughly 100 editors and guests in total and opted to host the show in his men's store on Madison Avenue. In addition to that, Ford did something people hadn't seen in the fashion industry before: he invited A-list celebrities to walk the show, many who had never walked in any fashion show before – or ever since. Julianne Moore, Beyoncé Knowles, Marisa Berenson, Lauren Hutton, Daphne Guinness, Emmanuelle Seigner, Rita Wilson, Rachel Feinstein, Lisa Eisner, Farida Khelfa and Lou Doillon walked alongside fashion's top models, including Joan Smalls, Liya Kebede, Amber Valletta, Daria Werbowy and Stella Tennant. Ford told the *New York Times* that none of the celebrities were paid to be in the show, though travel costs for a few were covered. But it perhaps did help that Beyoncé's husband, Jay-Z, was already a fan and customer of Ford's menswear collection.

While Ford's menswear debut had been more clinical and precise in its delivery, he made sure that his entrance into womenswear was filled with as much chutzpah and personality as humanly possible. He narrated the show himself, introducing each woman and describing the look that each one of them wore. The personality factor was all there, but so was the display of personal style for which Ford had become so well-loved when he was at Gucci and Yves Saint Laurent. Crisply cut suits in black silk and leopard print, sheer sexy blouses, expertly cut corsets, tasteful plumes of deconstructed

OPPOSITE Tom Ford's A/W 2018 men's collection was a mix of flamboyant suiting in pale pink and other hues.

LEFT Gucci's A/W 1996 jersey dresses were accented with metallic jewellery-like pieces; Tom Ford would carry on that opulent embellishment into his own line.

OPPOSITE Tom Ford's A/W 2018 men's collection included male models wearing only underwear and socks.

tulle and shimmering bodycon dresses were all there. Add to that, the Ford signatures of mixed hammered metal jewellery and sheer black stockings with a seam running down the back. Much like the menswear, prices were high, even for luxury products; at launch, the designer estimated the costs to be $3,500–5,000 for suits, $4,500 for a tuxedo, and up to $20,000 for a gown. Never mind the dollar signs: these were the house codes Ford started building at Gucci Group, which would traverse time and lead to the distinct DNA of Tom Ford the brand.

Adding to the strategic press approach to get as many people talking about Ford as possible, there was only one photographer allowed inside Ford's debut show. Terry Richardson, the photographer known for his sex-driven, provocative and often controversial photos, was the only one permitted to take pictures. Even for 2010, that was rare – this was right before the explosion of social media and long before the front rows would fill up with armfuls of raised phones. Ford intended to hold photos of the collection for a few months until releasing images on the brand's website.

2011 was the landmark year for Ford, when he continued to expand his namesake brand into womenswear. First Lady Michelle Obama wore a Tom Ford custom-made gown while visiting the British Royal Family. Rihanna and Lady Gaga were early adopters of the Tom Ford brand and would go on to wear some of the designer's looks for over a decade. In addition, Jennifer Lopez, Gwyneth Paltrow, Anne Hathaway, Ryan Gosling, Will Smith, Hugh Jackman and Jon Hamm are just a few others who have worn his designs.

Ford's womenswear venture seemed to be more global than his menswear debut. Following the Bergdorf Goodman men's retail partnership, the department store went on to be the second location to stock Ford's womenswear in New York

OPPOSITE The iconic Gucci G-string bikini, while now vintage, lives on in the canon of fashion history, forever influencing Ford's work.

City, with a devoted shop-in-shop which opened in September 2011. All the celebrity attention and a slew of successful runway shows meant that Ford had started to position himself as a global voice in fashion with a strong point of view.

The designer continued to pump out collections that referenced some of the very same themes from his early days – Disco! Pop! Art! Extreme glamour! Each collection was a cross-cultural slice of Ford's brain, fuelled by animal prints, sequins, spellbinding mesh and fashion that was all about the form – somehow all without being incredibly revealing or too salacious. Crystal-encrusted coats; floral spliced, wide-leg pants; leopard print fur-trimmed puffers; pink leather patchwork and suede-fringe masterpieces read like an autobiographical tale of Ford. A little bit Texan, a dash of New Mexico flair and a dollop of Gucci and Yves Saint Laurent's proclivities came together to form something that felt a little bit different.

By creating ready-to-wear alongside beauty, eyewear and accessories, Ford also solidified his business as the kind of big brand that people talked about and bought, as the price points for a pair of sunglasses or a perfume were far more accessible than a gown from the runway. By the end of 2014, for example, there were more than 100 Tom Ford stores around the world.

Ford would continue his work, until Estée Lauder Companies bought his brand in late 2022 for $2.8 billion. In April 2023, Ford announced he would be leaving the company as creative director, to be succeeded by his long-time associate Peter Hawkings.

OPPOSITE Brad Pitt was one of the earliest supporters and clients of Tom Ford's namesake line, seen here wearing one of the designer's suits.

TOM FORD BEAUTY AND LIFESTYLE

EXPANDING
THE EMPIRE

Beauty, as well as the overall aesthetic of lifestyle has always been intrinsic to the Tom Ford brand. When Ford was at Gucci and Yves Saint Laurent, alongside creating the visionary fashion for the two powerhouses, he also had a hand in creating the ad campaigns for fragrances.

When it came time for Ford to launch his namesake line in 2006, he knew he wanted to include beauty right off the bat. The first product launch was the Black Orchid fragrance, a scent originally intended for women but later also adopted for men. Housed in an inky-black bottle with textured glass and gold detailing, the fragrance would be a predecessor to the rest of Ford's beauty empire: it was incredibly strong, not for the meek, and ultra-luxurious, with a higher price point than other designer beauty lines at the time. Scented with notes of flora and truffles, it marked the beginning of everything. Estée Lauder famously once said, "When sex goes out of business, so do we," and in many ways, Ford lived by that motto.

OPPOSITE Today, the Tom Ford empire is inclusive of a full range of makeup.

ABOVE Tom Ford's full line of fragrances is known for being explicitly powerful and strong.

OPPOSITE Tom Ford's Black Orchid fragrance was the beginning of everything – the first perfume launched by the designer in tandem with his namesake brand.

"In the 1990s, it would have been a transparent bottle with minimalist packaging, transparent juice and a minimalist scent," Ford told the *New York Times*. "But we have become so dermatological in our approach to beauty that I wanted to put some glamor back into beauty with a powerful fragrance."

Ford partnered with Estée Lauder for backing – but it wasn't his first time working with the company. The previous year, he designed two makeup collections for Estée Lauder and reincarnated a classic perfume Youth Dew (his grandmother's signature perfume) as Amber Nude. Julia Restoin-Roitfeld, the daughter of Carine Roitfeld, starred in the campaign. By 2023, beauty, fragrance and eyewear made up the bulk of Ford's sales.

Some might say that the imagery Ford created on the beauty side was what fuelled the very va-va-voom, X-rated image that became so associated with Ford and his work. "I think fragrance might be more important than clothes," Ford has said. "Because, like music or food, scent is a very direct sensory stimulant. It provokes the senses, it brings up emotion and memory and feeling."

Even so, Ford was purposeful in his attempts to shock, and he pushed the envelope constantly when it came to beauty imagery. One such example is the Yves Saint Laurent campaign for the brand's Opium fragrance, released in 2000. The images show a sprawling Sophie Dahl wearing only jewellery and a pair of gilded leather high heels but otherwise stark naked, a fact both emphasized and carefully concealed by a high contrast, high-exposure effect. Shortly after that infamous campaign was released, Ford pushed the boundaries even more at Yves Saint Laurent with the campaign for the new men's fragrance M7. For the occasion, the ad displayed a black and white image of the martial arts star Samuel de Cubber reclining naked with his legs open and everything – yes, really everything – visible. "Perfume is worn on the skin, so why hide the body? The M7 campaign is really pure . . . it's a very academic nude," Ford said at the time. Both the M7 and the Opium ad campaigns garnered reactions and made headlines globally, with the M7 ad being called the first ad to ever display male full-frontal nudity.

Assembling a strong and directionally driven cadre of creatives who had a like-minded approach and an eye for all things controversial, Ford often worked with photographers who created sexually charged imagery, like Terry Richardson and Mario Testino. Carine Roitfeld, the stylist and former editor-in-chief of *Vogue Paris* was also brought on early as a collaborator to style Ford's Gucci runway shows and

continued helping Ford create sexy imagery through styling, skin exposed here, a hip bone showing there. In Roitfeld's reign at *Vogue Paris* from 2001 to 2011, the magazine was drenched in nude photography.

The nearly naked theme contributed to the Tom Ford beauty and lifestyle aesthetic for over a decade. Take, for example, the 2014 Neroli Portofino campaign riff with sensual innuendos. It starred Josephine Skriver alongside male model Jamie Jewitt,

with both models naked and intertwined in an oceanic setting. The same year, a 19-year-old Gigi Hadid who was then a new name to know, posed nude with just a bottle of Tom Ford Velvet Orchid perfume for the latest fragrance campaign, photographed by Mario Sorrenti.

Ford has always been interested in perfume, particularly in exaggerated scents that skew more baroque and rococo than timid and toned down. In 2007, he followed up Black Orchid with the introduction of his own premium Private Blend range, introducing 12 new scents, which are still in production today. Some of the bestsellers include Tuscan Leather, Oud Wood, Neroli Portofino and Tobacco Vanille.

Along with pushing the boundaries of imagery in beauty, Ford pushed just about every other angle he could imagine. His fragrances were often groundbreaking and set a new standard for high-end luxury fragrance connected to a fashion house. With the reign of minimalism, scents like CK1 were as good as gold, and Ford brought a new intensity, direction and attention to ingredients and quality to the table. He also pushed the limits with many of the names of his product. Case in point: the 2017 launch of Fucking Fabulous, a scent consisting of bitter almond, orris, leather, tonka bean and clary sage, which reportedly sold out in a single day when it first launched.

OPPOSITE Risqué beauty campaigns came naturally to Ford. While at YSL, he cast the model Sophie Dahl, pictured here, for the brand's Opium fragrance, wearing nothing but jewellery and boots.

THE TOM FORD LIFESTYLE

In 2011, Tom Ford launched makeup and in 2019, skincare. But even beyond beauty, Ford has done an excellent job of building out a formidable lifestyle aesthetic that matches the culture of his fashion and beauty products. Since he was a child, he loved moving furniture around, and likewise, as an adult, he's owned some of the most beautiful homes in the world.

LEFT Tom Ford seen posing with another one of his famously scandalous beauty campaigns.

Halston has always been one of the designer's biggest influences, so perhaps it comes as no surprise that Ford ended up buying the late designer's Paul Rudolph-designed New York City town house. Located on the Upper East Side, the chic futuristic home was recently revamped by architect Steven Harris. It's 650 square metres (7,500 square feet) with an epic glass façade and ultra-modern minimalistic design. Halston bought the house in 1974 and sold it just before he died in 1990 to Swiss photographer Gunter Sachs. In 2019, Ford purchased the home for $18 million.

Ford has made a habit of buying some of the most iconic homes across the country, building up his portfolio of real estate to rival some of the world's richest. He has owned and sold a quaint Victorian house in the London neighbourhood of Chelsea; a ranch in Santa Fe, New Mexico designed by Tadao Ando; and yet another iconic house, the Brown Sidney House, designed by legendary Austrian modernist Richard Neutra in Bel Air, Los Angeles. In 2019, Ford sold the Brown Sidney House for $20 million, having bought it in 1997, when he was in charge of Gucci, for just over $2 million. A hefty profit.

BELOW The lifestyle items – the iconic pair of Gucci handcuffs from 1998 – from Ford's tenure at Gucci are incredibly collectable.

One thing is clear: Ford loves all design aesthetics, and especially interiors. In 2016, he bought an Italian-inspired villa from the socialite Betsy Bloomingdale. Built in the 1920s in the Holmby Hills neighbourhood of Los Angeles, it's unique for being adapted in the style of the Hollywood Regency by Bloomingdale in the 1950s, designed by Billy Haines, interior designer to the biggest Hollywood stars. Ford's latest acquisition is a gem located in Florida: a house with 1,000 square metres (11,000 square feet) of living space on a one-acre lot in Palm Beach, which cost $51 million. Designed by Daniel Kahan, it's a contemporary modern palace fit for the king of glam aesthetics.

Even at the height of Ford's creative endeavours at Gucci and Yves Saint Laurent, he was not without his cheeky references or a hint of subversive ostentation. One of the best examples is the iconic pair of Gucci handcuffs from 1998, which are now incredibly rare. In 2017, they resurfaced on the second-hand retailer website Grailed, for $65,000. These chunky silver-toned Gucci handcuffs were reportedly displayed in Gucci store windows on the same day that Patrizia Gucci was jailed for hiring a hitman to kill her ex-husband, Maurizio Gucci. They're made entirely out of solid silver, weighing in at approximately 277g (8oz).

Some might say Ford himself was a master at creating a total vision for lifestyle. Note the way he dresses – always in his immaculately tailored suits and aviators – and also the way he controls his image. He has often appeared in his own campaigns, for example. And he has given us some equally theatrical moments during his finale bows at his shows. Take, for example, his Gucci show in 2004, his last for the brand. He wore a gardenia as a boutonnière, rose petals rained down from the sky and the soundtrack blared 'Nothing Compares 2 U'. Apparently before he left Gucci, he requested that the atelier make some things for him: a custom suit and a custom pair of tennis shorts.

OPPOSITE Tom Ford created lifestyle items such as the Yves Saint Laurent spring 2001 leather cigarette case and lighter, pictured here.

THE TOM FORD
AESTHETIC

DEFINING
THE BRAND

Ford, especially in his work at Gucci, is sometimes cast as a
minimalist, but the truth is, he's so far from it. While much of his
early work for Gucci and Yves Saint Laurent may be considered
tame compared to the Tom Ford aesthetic of today, Ford brought
forward a new kind of out-there glamour that heavily riffed on
1970s style at a time when copious designer houses were focused
on streamlined designs with little ornamentation and even less to
do with prints and colours.

Still, to understand Ford's total aesthetic it's essential to
appreciate that above all else, he has always been honest about
his commercial instincts. He says he went into the business to
"make women beautiful", through designs that are made to show
off and flatter the body. He firmly believes in the idea of fashion
not being cerebral; of it being rooted in pragmatism and instinct.

What's also important to understand about Ford's work is his
obsessive attention to detail, as well as just how hands on he is.
Take, for instance, the fact that in 2004, as the creative director of

OPPOSITE Tom Ford isn't afraid of colour – he often used it in big
doses with eccentric prints in his namesake collections for both
women and men.

Gucci, he personally shaved a "G" into the pubic hair of model Carmen Kass for an ad, adding definition with an eyebrow pencil. The Advertising Standards Authority fielded countless complaints from the ad while the watchdog group Mediawatch tried to get the campaign banned.

The lifestyle and campaign imagery from Ford's work at Gucci, YSL and for his own brand will always represent the provocative side of his aesthetic. Ford wasn't always like this, in fact, it seems like he grew into it. His first campaign for Gucci saw Amber Valletta wearing the same silky blue undone button-down shirt Madonna wore to the MTV Music Awards in 1995. Shortly after, the ads would show women being groped and in various states of undress, mostly photographed by noted collaborator Mario Testino. Georgina Grenville wore a demure wool sweater and pants, paired with an excessively large shining silver belt in the Fall 1996 campaign, as she is shown with a male model's hand snaking down her shirt. "Advertising campaigns became more exciting than editorial. When I started doing Gucci with Tom Ford he pushed me to new heights. He was, like, 'I've seen you do better than that. Don't get worried because it's a campaign,'" Testino told the *Independent* in 2008.

In many ways, Ford's hypersexualized imagery and branding would become the blueprint for an entire generation in fashion. The trickle-down effect could be seen in the ad campaigns of American Apparel and Abercrombie & Fitch among others. Both companies had provocative and controversial aesthetic styles – but then so did the photographers Ford worked with, including Terry Richardson and Mario Testino. This trend followed countless other contemporary fashion brands through the early to mid 2000s, almost all the way up until 2017 when the Me Too movement reached a fever pitch.

RIGHT Animal prints, like the zebra-printed dress seen here, are key to the Tom Ford universe.

LEFT There is a sense of dynamism in Tom Ford's work: the minimal shapes, muted neutral tones and sexy, body-hugging silhouettes he built at Gucci remain a core part of the Tom Ford visual identity.

OPPOSITE Aviator sunglasses are a favourite of Tom Ford, both the man and the brand – seen here in his early work for Gucci.

OPPOSITE Tom Ford heavily utilized pinstripes in his early work for Gucci.

RIGHT Another pinstripe suit look from Gucci's S/S 1996 collection.

According to Ford, he's always been particular. And that kind of hyper-specific attention to detail has come through in unexpected ways in Ford's work. Take, for example, the classic Tom Ford label: a rectangle with pointed triangular edges on either side, it resembles the same shape of labels usually associated with French haute couture.

Much of the brand has also been highly autobiographical to Ford. Take, for instance, the fact that Ford took inspiration from a pair of urns bought by his husband in Paris years ago, and he had them copied for the first men's store, and later, his stores all over the world. He took furniture and the things from his life that he loved and translated them.

There are certain iconic pieces that Ford created early on which will always be associated with the Tom Ford aesthetic. One such example is the Gucci's metal G-string from the Fall 1996 collection. The model paraded on to the spotlit runway with little else. She wore the interlocking G-logo G-string with sweater, shoulder bag and ankle boots. If you ask many fashion fans about Ford's Gucci era, many will think of this piece, for its representation of what Ford did for Gucci and what he defined as his future aesthetic. There would later be hints and references of it when Ford put his menswear models in underwear on the runway. Even decades after he left Gucci, it would remain an iconic style and insignia of Ford's emblematic style, and the G-logo thong silhouette was re-released as a bikini in 2022.

Hedonistic is a word that is often used to describe Ford's work. But something else about his aesthetic is that it's also particularly American. He represents the boldness, the grittiness and also the ambition. During the time he was in Europe in his early days working at Gucci and Yves Saint Laurent, he was one of the few Americans in charge of a global European fashion brand, and this set him apart stylistically and metaphorically. Maybe that's also the reason why he served as the chairman

OPPOSITE Tom Ford's namesake womenswear line often comes heavily embellished, with sparkling sequins, chunky beads and floral motifs.

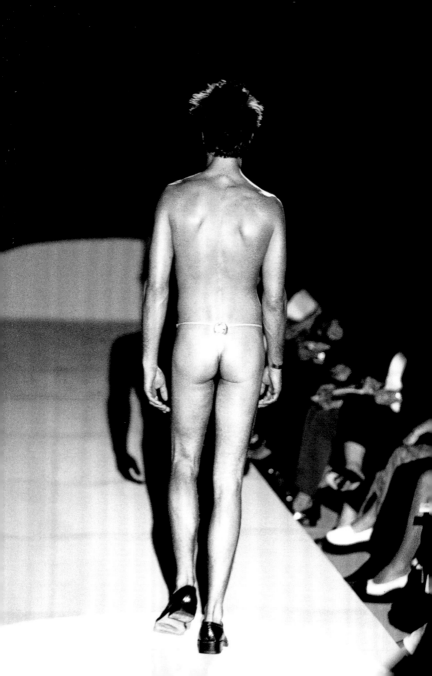

OPPOSITE A look at the infamous Gucci G-string designed by Ford.

RIGHT Rich, jewel-tone colours in silk and velvets are a signature of the designer – seen here on the runway and later worn by Madonna.

of the Council of Fashion Designers of America from 2019 to 2022. During his tenure, he launched the CFDA's A Common Thread initiative with *Vogue*, which donated over $5 million to the fashion industry in the United States. His tenure was unique in that it overlapped during a particularly difficult time in the industry – the pandemic – yet he helped usher both New York Fashion Week and the Met Gala back to life in 2021 and 2022.

Ford has commented on the preconceived notions of American style in the past, citing: "The truth is, Americans are afraid of style. We are descended from Puritans, and it is still in our culture. You can put an American woman and a French woman in the same clothes, and the French woman will just look different. The French woman's hair will, perhaps, not be as clean. She'll tie her scarf in a different way. She'll stand differently. But she'll look chic. The American woman will be too clean. That's the Puritanical strain. And too clean is not sexy."

But Ford, in that vein, also reinvented a new version of American sexed-up glamour. Look at his early work for Gucci and see the chunky silver hardware and jewellery – which is so clearly tied to the cultural aesthetic and influence of New Mexico, where he grew up as a child. The Tom Ford Fall 2013 collection was also inspired by New Mexico. With its flurry of dizzying prints, Ford called the collection "cross-cultural multiethnic". He designed the entire thing from New Mexico and included Native American motifs and Mexican aesthetic references.

Ford has said that his womenswear collections are largely inspired by two women who are his muses and friends: Carine Roitfeld and Lisa Eisner. Roitfeld, the French stylist, for the minimal European side of his work, and Eisner, the Los Angeles photographer, book publisher and jeweller who is influenced by the American West, for the over-the-top and bohemian fuelled collections.

OPPOSITE Tom Ford with one of his inspirations, the maximalist jewellery designer Lisa Eisner.

LEFT An important inspiration for Tom Ford, the French editor and stylist Carine Roitfeld.

Elsewhere, consider the overdose of embellishments like sequins, colliding colours, mirrored surfaces, exposed skin, bright velvet suit jackets and fashion show runways that look like the Hall of Mirrors at Versailles. They scream Texas, where everything is bigger and gaudier. "I also love the bold, unapologetic style that many Texans have," Ford once said. "My grandmother had that, and I still think that she was one of the chicest women that I have ever known. She was not afraid of style and loved clothes."

When it comes to menswear, the campaign side of Tom Ford has been no less flashy than its womenswear counterpart. But the clothing is slightly toned down, and even perhaps a little bit less referential of American glamour. His menswear suits, for instance, have been said to take inspiration from the British cut of a Windsor suit, with more suspension around the waist for even more of a fitted look than a traditional Savile Row suit. In other words, just like his womenswear pieces, these are suits that are made to stand out, but in a more subtle way.

Ford has been adamant that his menswear is about quality first and that he believes that menswear evolves at a much slower pace than womenswear, allowing him the time to develop ideas over the course of multiple seasons rather than creating an entirely new narrative each season. Ford has also said that he designs for a version of himself and that he is his own muse when it comes to menswear. From the start, he partnered with Ermenegildo Zegna to produce his menswear, one of the best Italian tailoring companies.

For both men and women, no Tom Ford look is complete without eyewear. It is essential to the brand, and it's one of the reasons why Ford launched eyewear before clothing. You can often see sunglasses in the campaigns and on the runways. "It is very potent stylistically," he once said. "You can totally change the image someone projects by putting a different pair of sunglasses on them."

OPPOSITE Tom Ford's most extreme looks are heavily embellished, such as this disco ball-like glimmering pant and shirt set.

LEFT The English actor Idris Elba wearing a Tom Ford suit.

OPPOSITE Sequin-embellished hoodies, animal-print pants, sky-high heels and sunglasses – these are a few of Tom Ford's favourite things.

ABOVE Tom Ford at the Met Gala wearing his signature aviator sunglasses.

OPPOSITE Tom Ford's menswear collection also includes watches.

The closer you look at Ford's work, especially in his womenswear collections, the more apparent it becomes that it's not without its little bit of kitsch and novelty appeal. Take, for instance, the hot pink moulded breastplate and fluid skirt Zendaya wore to the 2020 Critics' Choice Awards. The look was first seen on the runway in Tom Ford's Spring 2020 collection. But in order to get it to fit Zendaya perfectly, the design team came to her house and used 3D scanning technology. It was a look so iconic that it is considered one of the major reasons for her ascension to style icon. That's the thing with Tom Ford – his clothing demands attention, taking celebrities above and beyond into new versions of themselves, seamlessly reflecting cinematic style and awarding them iconic status.

TOM FORD
MUSES

A-LIST CLIENTELE

From the very beginning, Ford surrounded himself with a cadre of endlessly iconic muses who fuelled his overzealous aesthetic for Gucci and Yves Saint Laurent as well as his namesake brand. These people would become key collaborators as well as serving as long-term inspiration for the Tom Ford empire.

One of his earliest muses was Carine Roitfeld, the icon of style, stylist and former editor-in-chief of *Vogue Paris*, who styled most of the imagery for Tom Ford's Gucci collections shot by Mario Testino – injecting her signature hint of provocation. The duo would go on to have a longstanding collaborative relationship. When they came together and Ford served as guest editor for *Vogue Paris*'s December 2010/January 2011 issue, the resulting imagery and content was so salacious that it reportedly contributed to Roitfeld's resignation from her role.

As well as choosing her to collaborate, Ford has taken literal inspiration from Roitfeld's aesthetic, which could conceivably be considered sexy, undone, minimalist and intrinsically French. "It was summer and it was very hot, and she was

OPPOSITE Carine Roitfeld has worked closely with Tom Ford, and her personal style has also deeply influenced the designer.

working on a shoot with Mario Testino," Ford says, when he first met her. "She was wearing gray pants made out of Lycra T-shirt material with a narrow elastic band, and a very skimpy top. She also had on a pair of high heel slingbacks and was stepping on the back straps. I was in love the moment I first laid eyes on her; I even did a show where all the girls wore slingbacks but stepped on the back straps, as an homage to the first time I met her."

Early on, Ford also took a page from the Studio 54 scene that raised him, making Halston a long-term muse that he would refer to for decades – even buying Halston's former home in New York City. The 1970s silhouettes and overdose of extreme glamour was inspired by Halston. "I went to Halston's house one night when I was drunk and he made us eggs," Ford once said. "And I knew all these people like Bianca Jagger – I still know them – who look at me now and say, 'When did I first meet you?' I was just a 17-year-old kid who was dating a friend of theirs, but I was taking it all in. I was exposed to a lot of things that really did permanently mold my aesthetic."

But perhaps the unique power that Ford holds is being able to work collaboratively with many of his muses, rather than simply dressing them for the red carpets like so many other designers do. For example, Ford launched his first women's ready-to-wear show by enlisting A-list celebrities to walk the runway as models rather than to sit and watch from the front row. Julianne Moore, Beyoncé Knowles, Marisa Berenson, Lauren Hutton, Daphne Guinness, Rita Wilson and more walked the runway in Ford's new creations.

There are other ways in which the work of Ford went beyond muse too. Take, for instance, the aforementioned Beyoncé and Julianne Moore. Both have become important to Ford for different reasons. Moore starred in Ford's 2009 film *A Single Man* and routinely wears his designs on the red carpet – plus,

RIGHT Proving he also has a knack for classic, subdued glamour, Tom Ford has dressed the former First Lady Michelle Obama.

Ford even wrote her part in *A Single Man* especially for her. "When I first met Tom, it was in 1998; it was the first time I was nominated for an Academy Award," Moore told *Vogue*. "My baby was two months old. I wasn't really in Tom Ford shape. I came into the Beverly Hills Hotel and I was really nervous because I was going to meet this giant of American fashion, and here I am with my baby. The first thing Tom did was pick up my little boy – who's now 21 – and said, 'I want one of these.'"

Beyoncé as a muse stemmed from Ford's friendship with her husband, Jay-Z, who was one of Ford's first most devoted menswear customers when the brand launched. The two are so inspired by each other, in fact, that Jay-Z's 2013 album *Magna Carta Holy Grail* dedicated an entire track to Ford, repeatedly rapping his name in the chorus: "I don't pop molly, I rock Tom Ford". Ford was so inspired by the song he wanted to create a piece that would have icon status. What came next was a sequined dress referencing the jersey worn by Jay-Z while performing the song, the word "Molly" crossed out beneath the number 61.

As of 2021, Ford claimed that he has never paid any of his celebrity muses to wear the brand. He has also said that one of his all-time favourite celebrity red carpet moments was when Gwyneth Paltrow wore his white cape to the 2012 Oscars. Ford, unlike many other designers, has a history of not making custom pieces for his celebrity muses. Instead, he prefers they choose things directly off the runway, with only slight modifications. Examples include stage costumes made for Rihanna, Lady Gaga and Beyoncé. Rihanna, for instance, took a look directly from the 2013 runway and wore it to the Met Gala. There have been a number of menswear muses throughout the Tom Ford dynasty, but they're often much more understated than Ford's flashy womenswear. A few of

OPPOSITE Jennifer Lopez often wears Tom Ford, which blends seamlessly with her over-the-top glammed-up look.

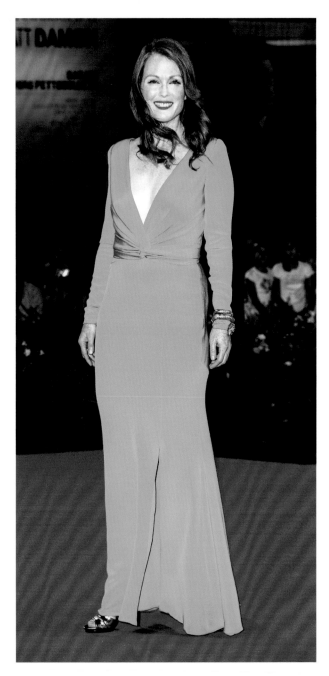

LEFT Julianne Moore is often dressed by Tom Ford in vivid shades of green.

OPPOSITE Moore also indulges in the designer's menswear-inspired suiting.

the menswear muses in the Tom Ford universe include: Daniel Craig who opted to wear Tom Ford in his final four James Bond films. Justin Timberlake who wore Tom Ford on his 2013 tour and André Leon Talley, who collected an assortment of custom Tom Ford capes to wear on the red carpet and elsewhere in full display. Brad Pitt was also one of the first celebrities to wear Tom Ford menswear almost as soon as it launched, followed by forever favourite fans including Drake and Tom Hanks.

These menswear muses proved that the Tom Ford man wasn't just one kind of aesthetic either. For Ford, dressing Timberlake for his global tour was an entirely new kind of opportunity when it came to scale. Ford designed over 600 pieces for the tour – totalling more than half a million dollars. He created pieces for the singer, plus his team of back-up vocalists, dancers and more. In addition, Ford also created eight brand-new, entirely custom suits.

Ford has been adamant about the connection to Hollywood and fashion, perhaps more so than many other contemporary fashion designers. He has said that global fashion is filtered through the lens of Hollywood, and in today's celebrity culture, Hollywood's influence is the greatest of all. When he opened his first menswear boutique, it was even inspired by his Hollywood muses. He wanted to create a Hollywood version of visiting a personal tailor.

Perhaps from a more personal aspect too, Ford found a muse in his long-time partner, the late Richard Buckley, who passed away in 2021. Buckley was already established in the fashion industry prior to meeting Ford, working as a journalist. In Buckley, Ford found a life partner, but also someone who gave him support – a long-time key figure in the fashion industry, Buckley was an editor at the industry titan *Women's Wear Daily* (*WWD*) and would go on to serve as editor-in-

OPPOSITE Fit for Queen B – Beyoncé has been a fan since the beginning, choosing some of the designer's most eclectic designs.

chief of *Vogue Hommes*. He could offer up his own opinions and advice, on everything from Ford's next business move to specific choices when designing collections.

Ford met Buckley in 1986 at a fashion show, but he would meet him again, not long afterwards, at the *WWD* offices. The relationship was quick, mired in passion, and the two moved in together not long after they originally connected. Ford and Buckley lived their lives openly as gay men with ease, defying conventions and stereotypes – rare, especially during the early years of their relationship.

Buckley's work as a fashion journalist and editor was referential of politics, culture and art and likewise, we can see a lot of parallels to the way Ford has approached fashion. Not just at Gucci and Yves Saint Laurent but for his namesake line as well. Buckley was with Ford from his very earliest career moments up until Buckley's death. Take, for example, the fact that he was there with Ford when he first moved to Europe for the brand-new Gucci gig. "With Richard in his life, Tom was able to soar," Anna Wintour wrote in an email to the *New York Times*. "Partly this was because of their differences." In 2012, Buckley and Ford became fathers, with the birth of their son.

Shortly after his son Jack was born, Ford produced one of his most colourful collections of all time for Fall 2013, inspired by Rihanna as well as Jack. Ford was an early supporter of Rihanna, long before she was considered the powerhouse global style icon that she is today. "I am sick of minimalism," he told *WWD*. "I'm not only sick of it in clothes. I'm color-starved. I don't want to do the obvious thing and all of a sudden attribute it to having a child. But having to decorate [Jack's] room in a color was really hard and now that he's here, I find that I don't have nearly the aversion. There's a hot pink room in one place, a bright orange in another house, a chartreuse room in another house."

OPPOSITE Actor Gemma Chan wore a silver Tom Ford gown and matching headpiece to the Met Gala in 2019.

LEFT The drama of Tom Ford's designs suits performers with big personalities, like Lady Gaga, seen here.

OPPOSITE Rihanna prefers to wear some of the most extreme looks offered by Tom Ford, straight from the runway.

OPPOSITE Singer Justin Timberlake is one of Tom Ford's menswear muses and has been dressed in custom suiting by the designer while on tour.

RIGHT Richard Buckley, the American journalist and Ford's life partner, was also one of his biggest muses.

LEFT For the Met Gala 2012, Rihanna wore a long black, crocodile embossed gown by Tom Ford.

But, interestingly enough, perhaps the biggest muse of the Tom Ford brand is himself. Ford has often placed himself in his own ad campaigns and on the covers of magazines under his own guest editorship, and it's easy to see how some of the models on his runways look like him. The 70s style aviators that have saturated his collections are a clear nod to the ones he wears himself.

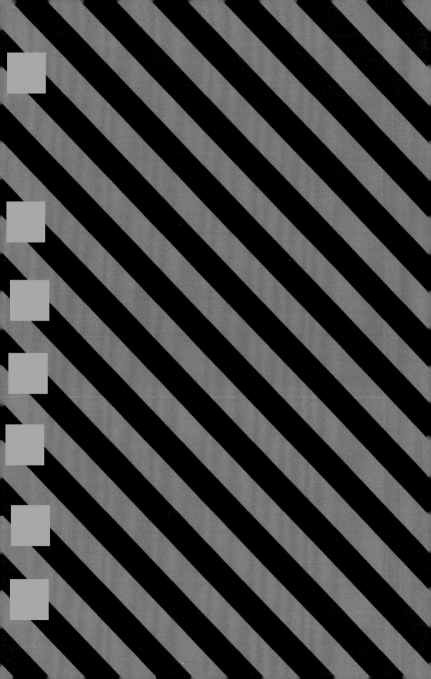

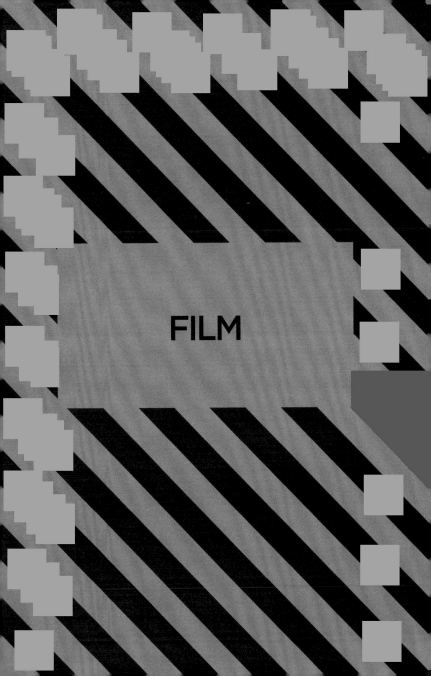

FILM

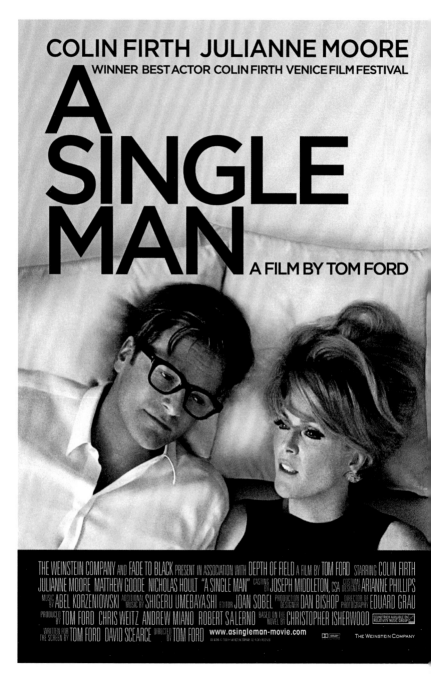

FASHION TO FILM

Tom Ford has never been just a designer. His connection to film, in fact, has always been intrinsic, and he has often cited hedonistic cinematic magic throughout his collections. Arguably, he first dipped his toes into film in a different sort of way, by designing costumes for some of Hollywood's most-watched screen deities.

Very shortly after leaving Gucci, in March 2005, Ford announced the launch of his film production company, Fade to Black. Ford's first official film was *A Single Man*, which he wrote and produced under Fade to Black, released in 2009. Based on the novel *A Single Man*, written in 1964 by Christopher Isherwood, the film stars Colin Firth as George Falconer, a sensitive gay professor contemplating suicide after his long-time partner dies in an accident, and Julianne Moore as his friend and former lover. Ford bought the rights to it along with a script by David Scearce, then rewrote the script himself, 15 times over the course of two years. Due to the global turbulent financial situation at the time, Ford's original financing fell through. Against his agent's advice, he decided to finance the project himself, allowing for complete and total creative control.

OPPOSITE Tom Ford's debut film featured his friend and close collaborator Julianne Moore.

As expected, Ford pushed the boundaries of clothing and narrative on the big screen. One case in point is the way that George Falconer carefully arranges his suit to attend a funeral. Ever the meticulous aesthete, Ford was incredibly hands-on in the film, even down to styling George's neat and grid-like drawers, which were inspired by Ford's own home decor.

Deeply personal to the point where it hinges on autobiographical, Ford isn't just hands-on when it comes to set design and the peculiarity of clothing, he also injects himself into different parts of his work in film. "The movie was so personal, and I grafted so much of myself onto the character of George, that I thought, 'If anybody ever wanted to know what Tom Ford was really like, all they have to do is watch that film.' Every bit of my being is in that movie," he said of *A Single Man*.

Ford's second film, *Nocturnal Animals*, was released in 2016 and based on Austin Wright's 1993 novel *Tony and Susan*. Ford once again self-funded the project to have creative control over every aspect. Starring Amy Adams, Jake Gyllenhaal and Michael Shannon, the visual language in the film is just as strong as that in *A Single Man*. It follows an art gallery owner who begins to re-evaluate her current relationship as she reads the new novel written by her first husband. Ford has also admitted that he sees parts of himself throughout the film, between the characters played by Adams and Gyllenhaal.

Ford's two film projects parallel each other in that they also both look at art – but the approach of film-making is perhaps what sets Ford's films apart from his fashion. "I'm a commercial fashion designer, I'm about things that sell," Ford told *Vulture*. "Making a film, for me, is the closest I will get to being an artist. I don't do it to live – this sounds spoiled, but I have money that comes from other sources. I do it for passion. I do it because I love it, which is also why I couldn't work with a studio controlling this. So I am more vulnerable,

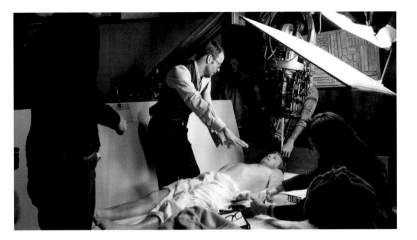

because when you care about something, you're going to be vulnerable."

Still, Ford has been vocal about the similarities to creating film and fashion throughout the years. For him, it's all about the vision and he insists that one has to have a very strong vision of the story one wants to tell and why one needs to tell it. He has often compared his experience of working with Gucci, with hundreds of people, to working on set collaboratively with hundreds of people, from set directors to lighting specialists.

Ever the perfectionist, perhaps that is why film suits Ford so well. After all, he has been cited as saying that being a film director is the closest thing to playing god that a creative person can have. Ford feels that fashion lacks some of the permanence that film has, in that film is forever, there's also the total control of the characters and whether they live or die.

Given Ford's precise and curated tastes, one might automatically assume that he also designs the costumes for his own films. But he doesn't. Rather, Ford selected celebrity stylist and costumer Arianne Phillips to dress the characters for both of his cinematic

LEFT Despite his interest, Tom Ford doesn't do the costumes for his own films.

LEFT The film *Nocturnal Animals* had a distinctly Western vibe, appropriate for a designer who is a native Texan.

ABOVE Arianne
Phillips designs
the costumes for
Tom Ford's films,
working to create
wardrobes that
feel authentic
rather than high
fashion.

projects. Best known for dressing Madonna on stage, Phillips
has also worked on the sets of well-known productions such as
Hedwig and the Angry Inch, *Walk the Line*, *Kingsman: The
Secret Service*, *Girl, Interrupted* and *3:10 to Yuma*. She's tackled
almost every visual aesthetic, from Western to glam rock.

Working as more of a cultural anthropologist than a traditional
film costume designer, Phillips's process of working with Ford
on his film productions involves careful character study. For
example, in *Nocturnal Animals* she explored two contrasting
facets presented by Ford: the elite, cultured Los Angeles gallery
world, as well as the dirty, gritty side of Texas (an element that was
autobiographical to Ford).

Phillips has long said that fashion in film is a reflection of
character, and she works with Ford to establish subtlety of
colour, fabrics, silhouettes and accessories to best express the
characters' intentions. In *Nocturnal Animals*, Adams wears
long white shift dresses, with clean minimalist gold and silver
jewellery – it's hard not to make linear comparisons to Ford's
early work at Gucci. The designer and film-maker was apparently
specific about the deep shade of green that Adams wore on

screen for cinematic pop. Adams's jewellery, by Lisa Eisner, came off as distinctly Western but somehow still cosmopolitan. On the other hand, Michael Shannon's costumes were all crafted from scratch because of their esoteric nature; firmly steeped in authentic Western culture, ten-gallon hats and all.

Of course, Ford being Ford means more access to great clothing than a typical director might have when producing any other film. Case in point: for *Nocturnal Animals*, Ford wanted Laura Linney, who plays Adams's mother in a flashback, to wear a Chanel suit. Unable to find one that felt truly and authentically 1990s, Ford reached out to Karl Lagerfeld, the then-former creative director of Chanel since 1983 – who custom-made a vintage-looking suit just for the occasion.

In *A Single Man*, Julianne Moore's character is supposed to be uninterested in fashion. Ford reportedly took inspiration from Moore herself, as well as his muse and friend, the jeweller and photographer Lisa Eisner and his grandmother, to lead Phillips into the costume design. Phillips went vintage shopping for the character, and came back with the perfect white and black dress. After Ford looked at the label, he realized it was from a little shop in Sante Fe, New Mexico, where his grandmother actually used to shop. That's just one of the many ways Ford puts himself in his films, whether viewers can pick up on it or not.

For Ford, it's clear that working in film will remain a big part of the personal brand he created, well into the future. "The most fun I've ever had in my life was making my two movies," Ford said, in his first exit interview since Estée Lauder Companies bought his company in late 2022 for $2.8 billion. The first film he wants to make post-sale may also be dark, as he told the press he wants to create "a dark comedy, because that's what life is. It's a dark, dark comedy. Life is just so much pain, but yet so absurd. I think if you don't approach it with a certain comedic point of view, it can kill you."

LEFT Tom Ford
self-financed
Nocturnal Animals
and *A Single Man*
in order to have
more creative
control – but this
didn't prevent
him from casting
A-listers, like Amy
Adams.

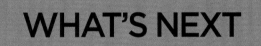

THE NEXT GENERATION

In April 2023, Tom Ford presented his Fall 2023 collection, his final for the brand he founded. Without all the ceremonial fanfare and eschewing the typical star-studded show, the collection was presented digitally, in the form of three short videos by photographer Steven Klein. The videos featured Ford's "favourite" pieces from the past 13 years: leopard print suits, metallic gowns, metal bustiers and sequin minis.

The collection closed with a series of all-black looks, rendered in lace, silk and croc-embossed leather. Of course, it wouldn't truly be Tom Ford without at least a little bit of a celebrity-studded send-off. Amber Valletta, Karlie Kloss, Karen Elson, Caroline Trentini and Joan Smalls all modelled in the videos.

Ford's final live runway show took place seven months earlier, in September 2022. The show closed out New York Fashion Week and was one of the most anticipated events of the season. Equally devoted to a palette of the label's greatest hits, it was also infused with quite a few references to Ford's archive of work, from the

OPPOSITE The fuchsia pink breastplate from Tom Ford's S/S 2020 show is one of the most iconic designs from the brand to date.

black satin bra tops à la Gucci Spring 2001, to the chiffon dresses alluding to Yves Saint Laurent Spring 2002.

A barrage of long-time models who worked with Ford over the decades walked in the show, along with contemporary stars, including Gigi and Bella Hadid. Many models sported disco ball-like glittering gowns that lit up the room like Christmas lights. Madonna, Ciara and Chris Rock were in attendance and many of the show's audience whispered that this show just might be Ford's last in-person show for his namesake brand, as the news that he was selling his company was swirling throughout the headlines. When models walked to the final song of Freddie Mercury's 'Time Waits for No One', there was truly an emotional feeling in the air, with a few veteran editors getting a little bit teary-eyed between claps.

Just a few months later, the news hit that Tom Ford sold his company to Estée Lauder Companies. And still the Tom Ford brand remains at its peak. In fact, some might say that the Tom Ford aesthetic has never been more in demand than it is now, with a rapid rise in the interest of archival fashion. Celebrities, as well as everyday fans of fashion, are rushing to collect and wear the designer's greatest hits out and about.

Some of the world's biggest names are showing support for all different eras of Ford's work. Take, for instance, the fact that Taylor Russell sported vintage Gucci by Tom Ford on the red carpet in 2022. In 2021, Rihanna donned rare Tom Ford-era Gucci pants from the Gucci Spring 1999 collection (available at the time she wore them for a cool $15,000, far above and beyond the original retail price). Kim Kardashian has worn Ford designs over the years too: she traded her usual bodycon dress for an oversized black suit by Tom Ford for Gucci at the 2017 LACMA Art + Film Gala. Fast-forward to 2023, and Kardashian wore a current season Gucci number that riffed on some of the references from Ford's early work at Gucci. The black dress, with cut-outs

OPPOSITE Tom Ford liked to switch things up for Fashion Week, doing everything from showing off-schedule, to showing underground, inside the New York City subway system, as seen here for S/S 2020.

LEFT Joan Smalls, Bella Hadid and Gigi Hadid seen backstage at one of Tom Ford's runway shows, with signature glam looks – smoky eyes, big hair, giant earrings and all.

and glistening "G"s across the hips, was a clear nod to Gucci's infamous harness skirt from Spring 1998.

In recent seasons, too, as the sale of Tom Ford was reported, it was speculated that the designer himself may return to his post as creative director at Gucci. That's because Gucci itself was reportedly going in a different direction. Alessandro Michele, Gucci creative director and ambassador of maximalism since 2015, suddenly exited his role in November 2022. According to industry source *WWD*, strong disagreements over the future of the brand caused a rift between Michele and president and chief executive officer Marco Bizzarri. In January 2023, Gucci announced Sabato De Sarno as its new creative director. His first collection debuted a month later, and one of the most powerful statements was a reissue of one of Ford's most striking bags: the horsebit clutch. Ford originally presented the bag in the Fall 2003 and Spring 2004 collections, magnifying the Italian fashion house's signature hardware and placing it on a neat little clutch, covered in everything from the label's classic monogram to its iconic red and green stripes and floral prints. The updated version for 2023 came in striking neon colours and proved that Ford's fashion is indeed timeless.

Many of the original Gucci pieces from the Tom Ford era are now harder to find and fetch high prices, regarded as unique in the canon of fashion history. In 2021, Ford himself admitted that he even paid $90,000 to add a dress he designed during his tenure at Yves Saint Laurent to his archive. "The clothes we make are not meant to be thrown away," he said.

The many pieces that Ford created for Gucci and Yves Saint Laurent now live on in a second life in the rare, archival space. Ford also created many cult-worthy pieces for the Tom Ford brand, which will soon likely receive a higher status in the fashion sphere now that he has left the brand. Pieces like a glittering Tom Ford logo jersey, a glittering pink bag that reads "pussy power", and a pink

OPPOSITE The sporty side of Tom Ford can't be ignored – metallic tracksuits are the brand's version of sweatpants.

LEFT Tom Ford
often presents
a handful of
men's looks at his
women's ready-to-
wear collections,
like this tailored
pink suit.

OPPOSITE There's been a surge of celebrities wearing Tom Ford's early designs – like Kim Kardashian, here wearing a black suit by Tom Ford for Gucci at the 2017 LACMA Art + Film Gala.

RIGHT Fashion favourite Taylor Russell chose vintage Gucci by Tom Ford on the red carpet in 2022.

metallic breastplate top already fetch more than they retailed for on second-hand resale websites and will probably only gain even more traction as time goes on.

In the meantime, we are in the new era of Tom Ford the brand, led by Hawkings, who most recently held the position of Senior Vice President of Tom Ford menswear, and who began his career at Gucci in 1998 (under Ford) before joining the Tom Ford brand in 2006. "In Peter Hawkings, the brand has found the perfect Creative Director," Ford said in a statement. "Peter began working with me 25 years ago as a menswear design assistant at Gucci and rapidly worked his way up to become the senior men's designer at the company when he left to join me at the Tom Ford brand."

Ford continued: "Since the creation of Tom Ford menswear, Peter has been instrumental in the success of the brand. He is an incredibly talented leader with tremendous industry experience, and his appointment gives me confidence that my commitment to creating fashion products with the highest level of design and quality will continue."

Guillaume Jesel was announced as the new president and chief executive officer, replacing Domenico De Sole, who held the position since the brand's founding. Jesel led Tom Ford Beauty since 2014, and his appointment proves a major emphasis on the beauty side of the business.

One of the achievements of the Tom Ford brand has been to make high fashion more understandable and appealing. Ford and, in the background, Hawkings have demonstrated how to take a fashion show and bridge the gap between the industry and the consumer. Case in point: in 2015, Ford was one of the first designers to schedule his show in L.A., timed to the Oscars, when a very different kind of crowd was eager for fashion and celebrities. It opened up the idea of a fashion show, giving it reach beyond the industry. In 2016, Ford was one of the first American designers to use the see-now-buy-now format, in which the clothing presented

OPPOSITE The mix-and-match maximalist menswear aesthetic of Tom Ford (seen here on the runway) continues to live on, with the brand's biggest fans wearing coveted pieces.

OPPOSITE Tom Ford for Gucci showed feathered jeans on the runway for S/S 1999. Rihanna wore them more than two decades later, in 2021, proving that great style is truly timeless.

RIGHT The glittery, shocking bags from A/W 2018 have become collector's items – speaking perfectly to Tom Ford's provocateur status. Could anyone else in fashion own such a bag moment as this?

ABOVE Tom Ford walks to take his bow at this runway show inside the subway.

OPPOSITE Perhaps one of the most iconic Tom Ford moments was when Beyoncé wore a sequined jersey from the designer – which cheekily referenced a lyric from her husband Jay Z's song 'Tom Ford'.

on the runway would be available immediately in-store rather than the typical six months later. Although this method has faded from popularity, the fact that Ford experimented with it early on showed that the brand is open to innovation. And in 2020, Tom Ford presented a runway show inside the actual subway system in New York City – another iconic and rare moment in fashion history.

While Tom Ford's own goodbye to the world of fashion may have felt unceremonious, the brand continues its tradition of groundbreaking shows, provocative clothing and impressive celebrities, led by new creative talent at the helm. Tom Ford without Ford has proved that the label is sticking to the many iconic house codes created by its originator. In the meantime, the world waits for Ford's own future cinematic projects, which will likely be injected with a great dose of his signature, curated aesthetics.

INDEX

CREDITS

The publishers would like to thank the following sources for their kind permission to reproduce the pictures in this book.

Alamy: Abaca Press 148; /Agf 72-73; / Matthew Chattle 69; /Cinematic 128-129; / Maximum Film 124; / Moviestore Collection Ltd 127, 132; /TCD/Prod.DB 130-131, 134-135; /Trinity Mirror/Mirrorpix 56; / Wirestock, Inc 66; /Katrin Zaitseva 67

Getty Images: John Aquino/WWD/Penske Media 6; /Bassignac/Benainous/Gamma-Rapho 28-29; /David M. Benett 46, 119; / Michael Buckner/WWD/Penske Media 74; /Martin Bureau/AFP 39; /Gilbert Carrasquillo/GC Images 104; /Mike Coppola 100, 149; /Pietro D'aprano/FilmMagic 101; /Gregg DeGuire/WireImage 98; /James Devaney/WireImage 120; /Fairchild Archive/ Penske Media 86, 87; /Giovanni Giannoni/ WWD/Penske Media 22, 25, 84, 85, 145; / Gotham 111; /S Granitz/WireImage 21, 43; /Francois Guillot/AFP 38; /Amir Hamja/ Bloomberg 48; /Patrick Hertzog/AFP 42; /Taylor Hill/WireImage 10-11; /Samir Hussein/WireImage 99; /Chris Jackson - WPA Pool 107; /Dimitrios Kambouris 108; /Stefanie Keenan/VF23/WireImage for Vanity Fair 93; /Brian Killian/WireImage 118; /Thomas Iannaccone/WWD/Penske Media 64; /Jeff Kravitz/FilmMagic 17 Inc; / Pascal Le Segretain 110; /Pascal Le Segretain/ amfAR15/WireImage 94-94-95; /Lexie

Moreland/WWD 142-143; /Kevin Mazur Archive/WireImage 14, 19; /Kevin Mazur/ Getty Images For Parkwood Entertainment 112; /Davide Maestri/WWD/Penske Media 24, 27, 50, 53, 90; /Patrick McMullan 9; / Jean-Pierre Muller/AFP 33, 34, 35, 36; / Victor Virgile/Gamma-Rapho 80, 83, 89, 96; /WWD/Penske Media 49, 54, 57, 138, 141, 151, 154; / Mychal Watts/WireImage for InStyle Magazine 70; /Theo Wargo/ WireImage 115; /Nina Westervelt/WWD 146-147

Heritage Auctions, HA.com: 40

Private Collection: 59, 75

Shutterstock: 153; /Matt Baron/BEI 117, 121; /Everett Collection 61; /Guy Marineau/Condé Nast 91; /Mgm/Columbia/Eon/Kobal 52; / Picturegroup 155; /Splash 152; /Startraks 116; /Steve Wood 41

wildwoodantiquemalls.com: 77

Kristen Bateman is a New York City-based writer, editor and creative consultant. She has authored five books and also writes for the *New York Times*, *Vogue*, *W* magazine, *Architectural Digest*, *Elle* and many other magazines. Her focus is on writing features about fashion history and trends beauty, culture and interiors. She also has her own jewellery brand, Dollchunk.